Jesus is Born!

Coloring & Activity Book

The Standard Publishing Company, Cincinnati, Ohio. A division of Standex International Corporation. © 1999 by The Standard Publishing Company. Bean Sprouts™ and the Bean Sprouts design logo are trademarks of Standard Publishing. All rights reserved. Printed in the United States of America. Illustrated by Len Ebert. Cover design by Rob Glover. Reproducible: Permission is granted to reproduce these pages for ministry purposes only—not for resale. Scriptures quoted from the *International Children's Bible, New Century Version*, copyright © 1986, 1988 by Word Publishing, Dallas, Texas 75039. Used by permission.
ISBN 0-7847-0995-5

Standard Publishing
Cincinnati, Ohio

06   05   04   03   02   01   00   99   5   4   3   2   1

God promised his people that Jesus would be born.

People prayed to God and waited for him to send Jesus.

God chose a special family for Jesus.

Find the names of Jesus' parents and some of his other relatives in this word search. Look up, down, across, and backwards.

MARY

JOSEPH

DAVID

```
Z A R U T H G O Q
P C B O D N C D H
D G T Q N G T Q P
A A B R A H A M E
V L T H S A F S S
I M D N A W G M O
D T M A R Y R S J
E V T O A G F K Y
R V H W H L J H I
```

RUTH

ABRAHAM

SARAH

5

The angel said to Mary, "God has blessed you!"

He said, "You will give birth to a son
and you will name him Jesus."

Mary praised God.

Joseph and Mary were engaged to be married.

Mary and Joseph went to Bethlehem to be counted.

Mary and Joseph went to Bethlehem to be counted. How many people can you count in Bethlehem?

Bethlehem was crowded.

There were no rooms left in the inn.

Help Joseph and Mary find a place to stay for the night.

That night Jesus was born.

**"She wrapped the baby with cloths
and laid him in a box where animals are fed."**
Luke 2:7

17

Three of the cows in this picture are exactly alike.
Can you find them?

In all the excitement, these animal families got mixed up. Draw a line to connect the baby animals to their mothers.

Make a 3-D picture!

Tear out page 23 and color the pictures on it. Carefully cut them out along the bold black line.

Next cut along the dotted line at the bottom of the page. Cut this strip of paper into 4 pieces. Fold the pieces up like an accordion.

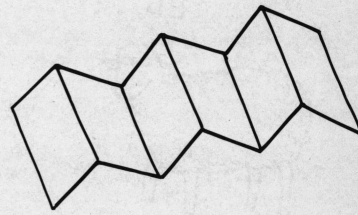

Tape one end of the folded paper to the back of the colored picture. Tape the other end to the picture on page 25.

"Some shepherds were in the fields nearby watching their sheep."

Luke 2:8

What are these shepherds watching over?
Connect the dots to see.

What's wrong with this picture?
Circle all the things that don't belong.

**The angels appeared to the shepherds,
and the shepherds were frightened.**

The angel said, "Do not be afraid. I am bringing good news!
Jesus was born today in Bethlehem!"

**The shepherds went quickly to see baby Jesus
and to worship him.**

Make a choir of angels!

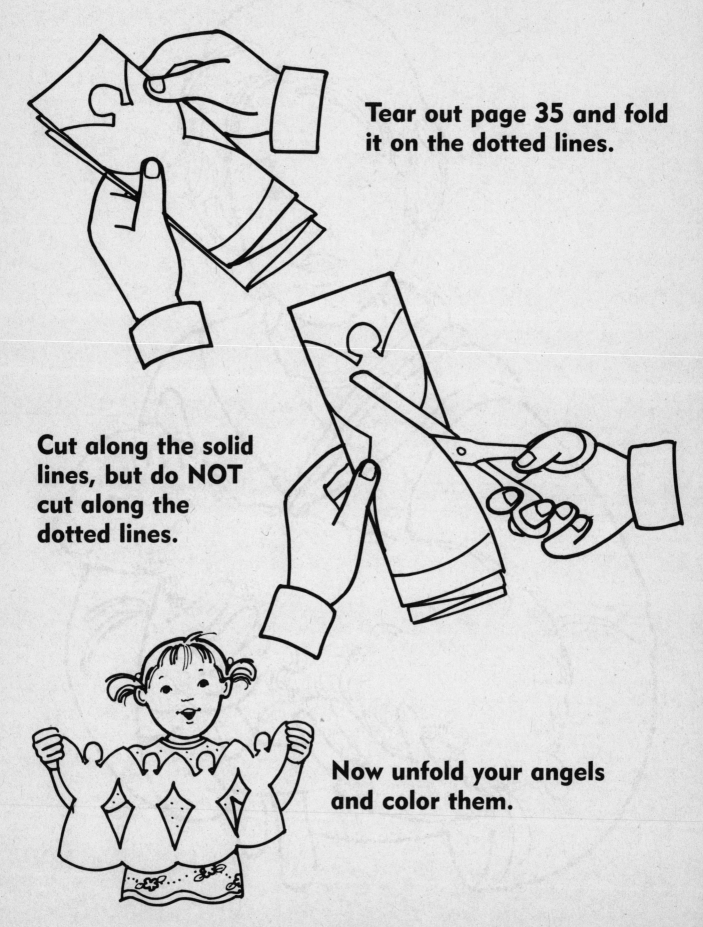

Tear out page 35 and fold it on the dotted lines.

Cut along the solid lines, but do NOT cut along the dotted lines.

Now unfold your angels and color them.

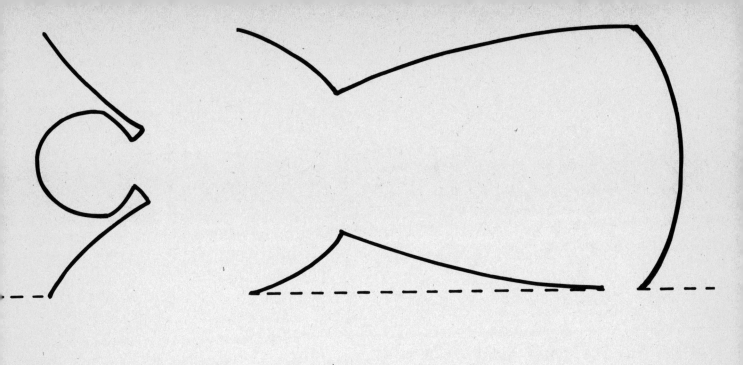

"Glory to God in heaven, and on earth let there be peace to the people who please God."

Luke 2:14

After Jesus was born, wise men from the east came to see him.

**The wise men said, "Where is the baby Jesus?
We saw his star in the east. We came to worship him."**

Connect the dots to see what the wise men were following.

This wise man lost his luggage on the road.
Draw in a new crown and a rich robe,
and give him a treasure for baby Jesus.

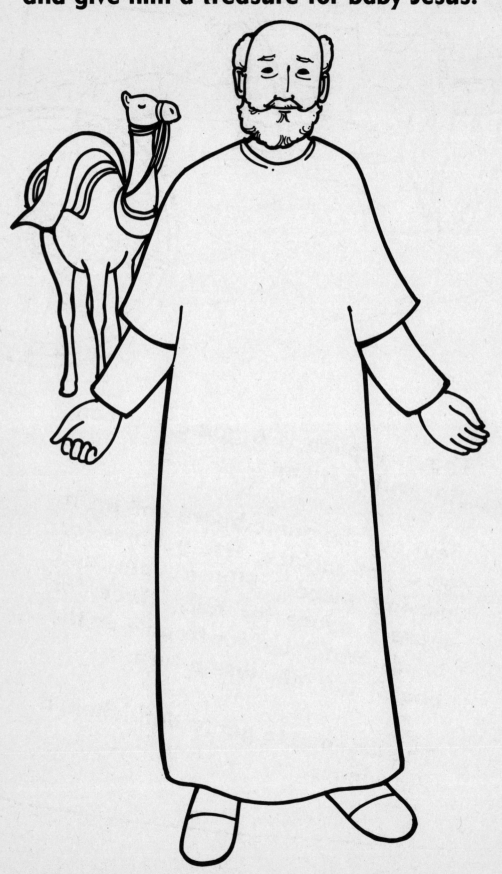

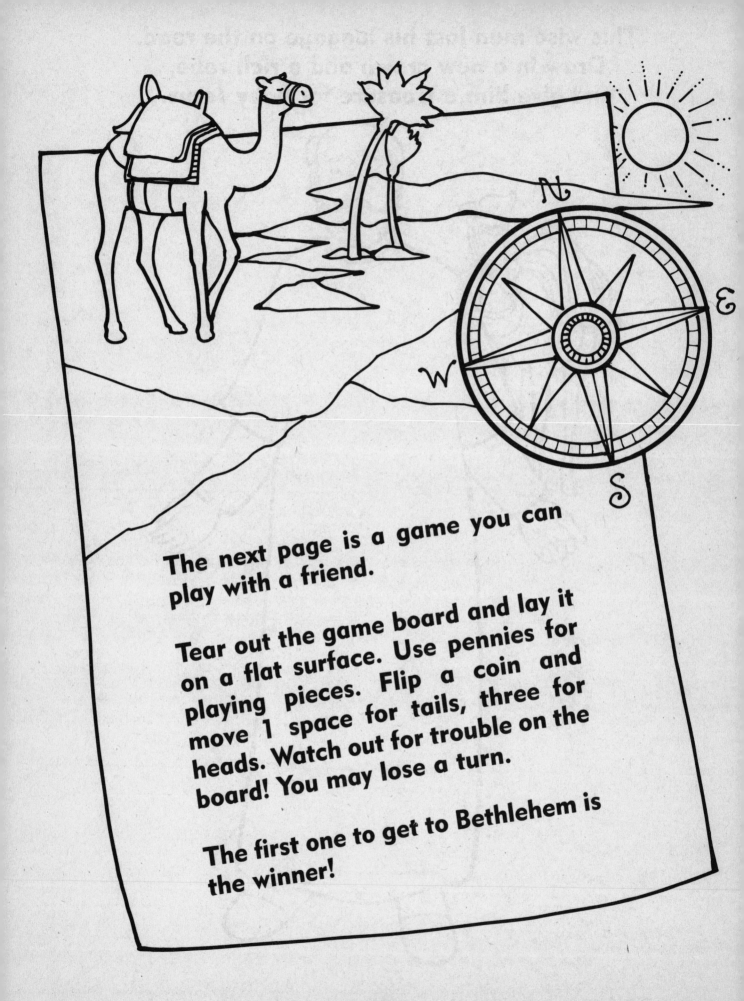

The next page is a game you can play with a friend.

Tear out the game board and lay it on a flat surface. Use pennies for playing pieces. Flip a coin and move 1 space for tails, three for heads. Watch out for trouble on the board! You may lose a turn.

The first one to get to Bethlehem is the winner!

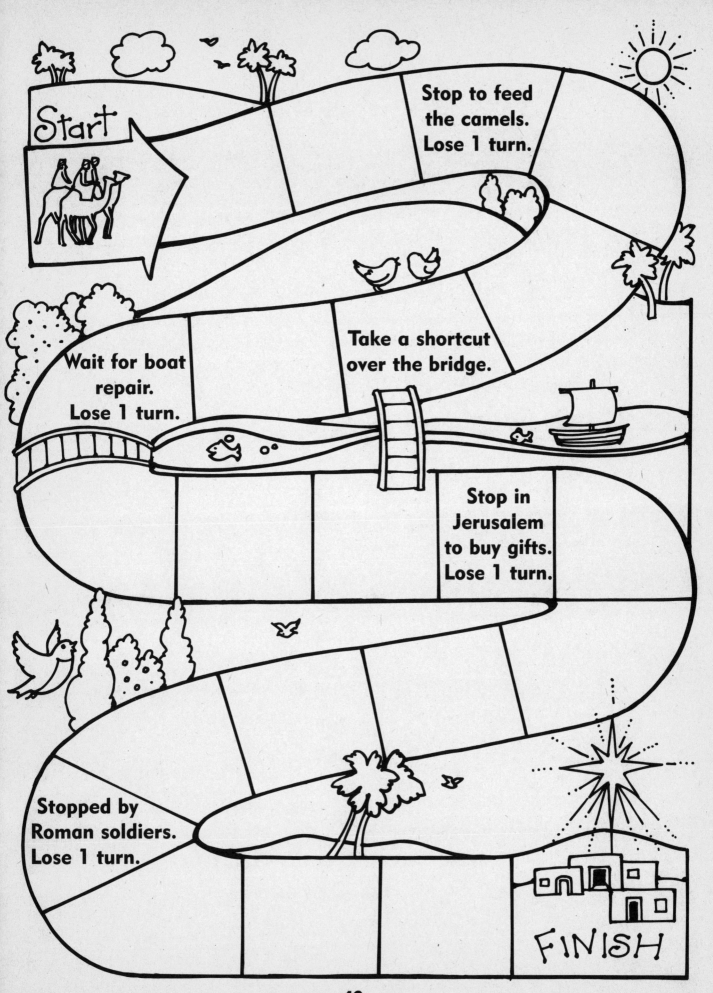

Start

Stop to feed
the camels.
Lose 1 turn.

Wait for boat
repair.
Lose 1 turn.

Take a shortcut
over the bridge.

Stop in
Jerusalem
to buy gifts.
Lose 1 turn.

Stopped by
Roman soldiers.
Lose 1 turn.

FINISH

Color the blocks to reveal a hidden picture.
1= yellow   2= black   3= blue   4= brown

The wise men gave Jesus treasures.

"Glory to God in heaven, and on earth let there be peace to the people who please God."

Luke 2:14